# NEWPORT TRANSPORTER BRIDGE AND INDUSTRY ALONG THE RIVER

Jan Preece

AMBERLEY

*This book is dedicated to my late wife Sally, my children, Jan, Jody, Tori, Anna, Lucy and Gemma, to Duncan and to my dear friend Yoasia.*

*Front cover*: Image courtesy of photoeverywhere on www.freeimageslive.co.uk.

First published 2019

Amberley Publishing
The Hill, Stroud
Gloucestershire, GL5 4EP

www.amberley-books.com

British Library Cataloguing in Publication Data.
A catalogue record for this book is available from the British Library.

ISBN 978 1 4456 7785 9 (print)
ISBN 978 1 4456 7786 6 (ebook)

Origination by Amberley Publishing.
Printed in Great Britain.

# Contents

# Introduction

I can't recall any part of my life that has not had a river, a coastline or a bridge in the equation. I look out upon the massive towers of the Newport Transporter Bridge, I hear the daily shrill of the gulls, always an hour into the falling tide, when the pickings are rich, and in my formative years I grew to hear and love the fuss of the tugboat, the deep throaty blast of the merchantman as it prepared for its sea journey or had entered the sea lock. I live in Pillgwenlly, the flat lands, bordering the River Usk and Newport's massive

ALEXANDRA NORTH DOCK, NEWPORT.

*Newport agrees with me splendidly, the people here vie one with the other in giving one a real good time.*

Most came in search of work during the years of industrial expansion when Newport, the most 'westerly port in England', shed its identity as a town of little importance and became a progressive port and centre of industry.

One of the oldest industries in the area can be seen in the remains of the salmon fisheries on the Severn at Goldcliffe, Newport.

Alexandra Dock. Running alongside the river, deep into Pillgwenlly, was the Newport & Brecon Canal, which brought with it even more deviation and history. Those within my community were seamen, coal trimmers, engineers, foundrymen, steelworkers and railway men. Few were indigenous, as Pillgwenlly was, until the late 1700s, just a small group of cottages on the Pill, belonging to Gwyllym.

A new period has begun. In this book we will look at the transporter bridge from a slightly different perspective and at some of the principle industries and communities once found on the banks of the River Usk.

To examine the past and the incredible story of the industrial growth of Newport, we first need to identify the key components that have brought us through time to the present. We will look at:

1. The growth of the canal
2. The railways
3. The River Usk
4. The docks
5. The transporter bridge
6. The industries on the river

Our unique transporter bridge has its own story to tell – in how it came to be and of those who have benefitted from its presence; in the community it served and the story of those whose livelihood came from the river; and in what it provided, whether it be coal, engineering, foundry or shipping

Jan Preece

# The Arrival of the Canal

In the seventeenth century, tram roads came to the ancient port of Caerleon, a little over 5 miles from the centre of Newport. The aim was to link the iron and tinplate works in the lower Eastern Valley to the old quayside, from where trading vessels had regularly sailed downriver to the channel. The tram road was extended beyond the town bridge in 1808.

However, anticipation that Caerleon would continue as a port had already been scuppered by the construction and opening of the Monmouthshire Canal in 1796. When completed, the canal was to have two arms – one from Newport to Crumin via fourteen locks, found off the main Newport to Risca Road at High Cross, and via Malpas and Cwmbran to Brecon in the opposite direction.

Tall ships could not operate this far upriver, which also sounded the death knell for Caerleon as a port of any modern importance. The colliery and foundry owners demanded a far more accessible outlet for their goods.

A milepost, dated 1822, states that it is 3¼ miles from the old bridge pier at Caerleon.

For the narrowboat men, Newport was the entrance to the Barrack Hill Tunnel, after which they were emerged into a different world – an ever-expanding melting pot of land reclamation and growth.

Pill, which was downstream to the town bridge, took up the sizeable triangular area upon which the Newport Central Market now stands. The canal basin, situated adjacent to this, was in fact Newport's first dock; this in its own right was a large area of water, which according to the early maps of that time was accessed via Skinner, Griffin, Market Street and the Old Green. Having this large dock right in the centre of the town, near the Market House (which was soon afterwards demolished) and the castle must allowed for a very exciting period in Newport's history. The canal also served the mill, the castle and in later years the gasworks. The castle has seen various uses over the years, including as a brewery. It did, however, lose part of its historic moat as many tons of soil were dumped into it during the construction of the canal basin.

A second Act, granted in 1797, allowed the canal to be extended from the centre across Pill, and a further Act, in 1802, allowed the canal to progress to a point known as Prothero's Wharf in Pillgwenlly. The Newport Central Market and adjoining streets were built on the ground reclaimed from what was the town of Pill and the canal basin, while the canal followed the path of the river, heading towards Pillgwenlly.

One of the first wharfs on the new extension is listed as Moderator Wharf, which was bordered by the canal on the town side and the river on the other. There was a drawbridge on the castle side of the canal, which allowed shunting engines to cross the waterway and could be lifted to allow the narrowboats to pass.

The meandering canal, about to enter Barrack Hill Tunnel. Taken during the construction of the inner ring road, the narrowboat men of the eighteenth century would have faced similar redevelopment and regeneration of the ancient borough as it expanded to meet the demands of industry.

There is no evidence of the canal here, in Shaftesbury Street, during the construction of the inner ring road in 1990, but it would have emerged here from the Barrack Hill Tunnel. For many years it shared its path with the railways, but has lay dormant since the late 1930s, when it was last used for commercial purposes. The canal has vanished, the railway has followed suit, and the road now reigns supreme. How dare it!

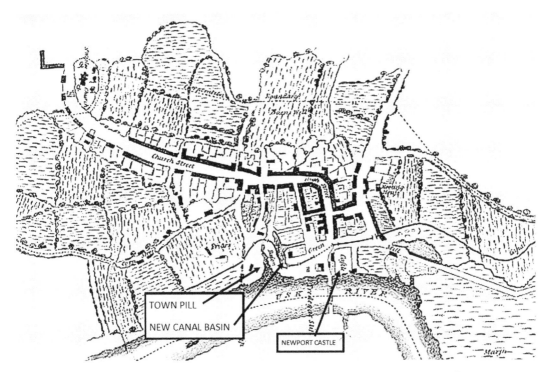

This early map, dated *c.* 1794–95, clearly shows the canal basin in relation to Pill.

Market Street (*c.* 1985), in the centre of Newport, would have been near the first canal basin. The style of the buildings is quite at home near a dock or canalside.

Here we see the scene from the opposite direction. The Market Hall, which was built over the Old Town Pill, stands proudly on what is now known as Upper Dock Street. This drawbridge is a definite improvement to the wooden cantilever seen in the previous picture. This was the age of the wooden cask, many of which are seen on the canal edge. On the left of the picture horse-drawn carts await their loads, no doubt to furnish the merchants and shopkeepers eagerly awaiting their supplies.

A narrowboat, which seems to be carrying various minerals, glides slowly under the drawbridge. The railways have clearly won the day, as all of the cargo held in the narrowboat could be carried in just one or two trucks. Nevertheless, this is a beautiful icon of the gentle days and a reminder of what some consider to be far better times.

## Across the Marshes to Pillgwenlly

If crossing Pill was difficult, then driving the waterway over the marshes to the lower reaches of the river must have had nightmarish ramifications. Pillgwenlly, which was still a village, was over 10 feet below sea level. It would take a mammoth act of civil engineering and manpower to complete the task.

Work began on this section in 1806 from Friars Fields to the Mellon Embankment. A new embankment was created and much pile driving was required to move forward and cross Jack's Pill. Thousands of piles, consisting of stone blocks brought from the quarry on Barrack Hill, were driven deep into the mud and the inner core of the Pillgwenlly Embankment. In 1808 the river was contained. It was more than just an embankment that was constructed, though, for with the canal came jetties, loading facilities and wharves.

In Newport, the changes in Pillgwenlly were racing forward as thousands of tons of ballast were dumped into the marshes. Thus, the watery wilderness known as Pillgwenlly was absorbed into the borough of Newport.

The Union Inn was built on the canalside at Jack's Pill in 1817. It was a landmark inn, representing the end of what could have been a most dangerous trek from the lodging houses of Newport to the canal working and, a few short years later, the commencement of the Town Dock. Immigrant workers who were unaware of the local geography failed to circumnavigate the horrendous conditions brought about by the marshland and the thousands of tons of ballast that were heaped everywhere. It is said that they followed the light across the marshes, and the crude track to the Union Inn eventually became the foundations of Dock Street.

Malpas Lock on the Newport/Cwmbran arm of the canal. The cabin and living quarters on a canal boat were little bigger than a small garden shed; the life of a boatman was not an easy one.

*Above*: Probably the last piece of substantial evidence of the canal in central Newport was this stone-built exchange building. The arch through which the canal passed can be clearly seen. Despite efforts to save the building, it vanished, passing into the history books – as have so many of Newport's historic buildings.

*Left*: The very last frame on the film – how I wished I had carried more. A scrounge around the Old Town Dock area in the early 1970s showed me the remains of the canal wall and what I believe to have been the Potter Street lock. Here, I was nearly at the extremity of the Pillgwenlly extension of the Monmouthshire Canal.

The Riverview Club, seen in 2016, and below is a similar view taken in 1974. The famous Octopus Bridge that crossed the line, allowing access to the old dock and the riverside, is still intact.

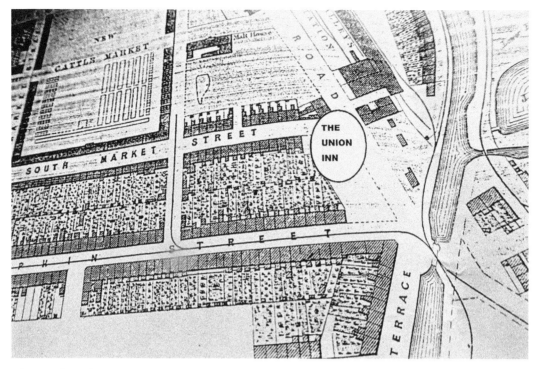

This is where the Union Inn once stood, on the footpath of the canal. It has always kept the identity of a hostelry, previously being the Richmond Hotel, and now is the Riverview Club.

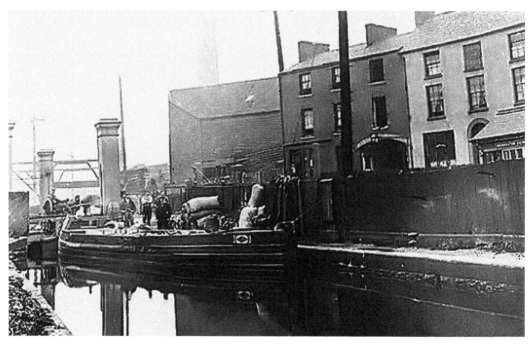

The last barge leaving Newport, probably photographed in the late 1930s.

Kings Parade, Pillgwenlly, where the canal would have terminated. There was a small basin at the end of the street to enable turning.

The end of the canal as a working waterway came as if someone had pulled the reversing handle. The Pill extension was the first to go, with it then withering slowly until the point where it ran under Barrack Hill. Much work has been done to preserve the locks and a navigational stretch from Cwmbran to Brecon, and there are currently plans afoot to link the whole system again by re-opening the Cwmbran stretch, where it has been covered over.

# The Railway

It was inevitable that there would soon be conflict and a fierce competition between the canal companies and the railways. By 1808 the riverbanks had been reinforced and the tide contained. The ensuing years were the golden years as far as the canal companies

Courtybella Junction.

were concerned, with the Monmouthshire Canal being one of the most profitable in the land. However, it was not all a bed of roses. Some years later, the *Monmouthshire Merlin* letters column made references to 'the canal companies' exorbitant rates of tonnage and the poor construction of their roads'.

Comparisons were being drawn with the faster, cheaper and more efficient railway. A rot was setting in; in fact, while the canal was being taken across Pill, another Act was passed to bring a tram road from Sirhowy to Newport, which came into being as far as Crumlin in 1808, and did not reach Newport until 1812. In spite of these misgivings, the canal functioned as a business alongside the railways until the 1930s.

The railway entered Newport via Courtybella Junction, which is on Cardiff Road adjacent to the excellent Belle Vue Park, and what were the Whiteheads and Godings steel plants. From here it threads a circuitous route along Cardiff Road and in the other direction, through the maze of streets towards the river, the canal basins and the docks.

At that time Dock Street station was the principle station for the town. It was roughly a mile from Courtybella, making the temporary platform there redundant. Its name suggested being intrinsically linked with the canal, the docks and the river, as at this time they all ran parallel to each other.

Stage two had been completed.

Waterloo Junction.

# The River Usk

Living on the water's edge is living next to an open window on the world. As each tide eddies and swirls around the muddy landscape of our coastline, it brings with it evidence of a bygone age, uncovers the often-buried wonders of the past – sometimes exposing a tantalising hint, other times presenting us with great gifts of knowledge and archaeological treasure.

At the point of entry from the sea, the very essence of a river is that of an aquatic highway. In the case of Newport, it was believed to be a safe and secure entry into the medieval borough, allowing valuable goods to be taken to the castle and, of course, onwards to Caerleon. The greatest evidence of this early trade was, without doubt, the discovery of the Newport Medieval Ship.

## The Newport Medieval Ship

By 2002, most of the old riverfront had vanished. It was during the construction of the new Riverfront Arts Centre that a number of ancient timbers were discovered in the mud. Nothing unusual in that, one might add, seeing as the river, as previously mentioned, is a storeroom of history. And it was planned to cover that area in concrete.

A small window was given to investigate and it was suggested that this was indeed a major archaeological find. The council were unmoveable in their plans, even though the timber was now confirmed as belonging to a medieval ship of some stature. Cover it in concrete and leave it for another generation to re-discover was just one daft suggestion.

Mr Charles Ferris, a local businessman, and myself, a heritage activist and author, decided to start a pressure group to save the ship. What ensued can only be described as unique and quite remarkable. It was agreed that a roadside vigil would be held at the site. Media coverage spread the story rapidly and the numbers grew. It was heart-warming and touching to be part of such a groundswell of passion for an object that had lain in the ground for six centuries. Food and drink appeared in abundance as local traders did their bit. In the middle of the night, hooded and anonymous faces arrived in boy-racer cars: 'Brought you some crisps and pop, all right? Cool!'

At the eleventh hour, a joint package of funding was found, and the Newport Ship began its next great journey, from dereliction to preservation.

All from a hole in the ground – timbers of a 400-year-old craft are slowly exposed from the thick river mud.

Seven days to go and the roadside vigil grows stronger by the day.

An incredible act of support came from the sea when a flotilla of small ships came upriver on the incoming tide to offer their support. It was indeed the Dunkirk spirit that had arrived on the banks of the River Usk.

The prize! Illustrated in this delightful painting by artist David Jordan is the Newport Ship as it might have been when it came to the shipyard on the Usk, which became her resting place for over 400 years. She was built by the Basques in 1450. Hundreds of artefacts have been discovered telling her story. The city of Newport and the Friends of the Newport Ship, along with archaeologists from the world over, have truly taken this to heart, allowing the project to flourish, even in these times of financial uncertainty.

The discovery of the Newport Ship has filled a gap in the history of ship repair and building on the Usk, and there were doubtless many smaller boat yards and craftsmen dotted along the banks.

What else is buried here in the mud is a matter of conjecture. Some of the team that made the initial discovery say there are more ships waiting to be found. I fear it would be a heart-stopping moment for Newport City Council should this journey begin again.

## The Temperamental Usk

The River Usk has the second highest rise and tidal fall in the world. At its lowest, the flow is often reduced to little more than a stream, with sandbanks becoming exposed and the river offering up its hidden treasures. In extreme storms, the waters run a muddy red as the soil from the fertile Usk Valley is washed away, sending red silt, trees and debris out into the open sea. This most temperamental of rivers has created many problems, one of which was crossing between the east and west banks. The other was extreme flooding. The adjoining land was frequently awash as the terrain in Pillgwenlly was below sea level.

Prior to the opening of the sea lock in the Alexandra Dock, access to both docks was via the river. The east lock entrance to the Alexandra North Dock was just south of the transporter bridge, while the entrance to the Town Dock was near to what is known as Spittle's Point – named after industrialist and foundry owner Thomas Spittle.

As the tide retreats, the distant sandbanks are exposed, often leaving stranded salmon in the mud pools.

## The Town Dock

The Town Dock had been built with a short feeder link to the canal. The canal basin at Pillgwenlly was almost at the water's edge. It had followed and had competed with the Usk through its entire journey from central Newport to its final cut. The railway drew it all together, a chaotic web of lines punctuating the streets, lanes and the water's edge, like a vast, poorly constructed knitted jumper.

The Town Dock, which we now refer to as the Old Town Dock, was completed in 1842. The millions of tons of materials being brought into the port via the tram roads and the canal was far more than the river wharves could cope with, so the building of a new dock was not only necessary, but inevitable.

A few years later, in 1858, the final stages of construction took place and a dock extension was added. Such was the extent of the celebration that a public holiday was declared in Newport, and even the SS *Great Britain* of Liverpool came to visit, being towed by a tug between the old and new docks. Sailors danced at the masthead and flags fluttered from the mainsail. What a sight this must have been! It is the norm to see archive images in black and white, but we must not forget – history was in colour!

Following many years of dereliction, the Old Town Dock is slowly coming back to life – not as a dock, unfortunately, but being scenically enhanced in places and bordered with modern housing. There is also a gastro pub near the sea lock, though imagining the

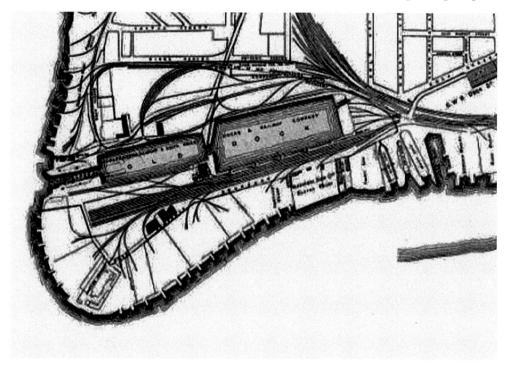

Map of the Old Town Dock, from an early *Docks Handbook*.

The Old Dock from an early engraving, the entrance of which was in the River Usk. Great skill was required to navigate the craft into the entrance locks. This was done by bringing the ship into a small area of still water prior to being winched into the sea lock.

The wonderful *SS Great Britain* came from Liverpool as part of the Old Dock extension celebrations. Here she is at her home in Bristol, undergoing a complete restoration.

A site of special scientific interest – the entrance to the Old Town Dock.

Science and hard work come together as massive sunken chambers are made ready for the gigantic transporter bridge.

The problems of the low-lying ground were once more in evidence during the redevelopment years, when the old foundations were excavated for the construction of new properties.

duel carriageway is not there and that you can see the sails on the river as you sit and eat is certainly wishful thinking!

The fragility of the area was highlighted in 1899, when a severe storm caused what was then called the 'Great Flood'. Ships broke away from their moorings and lives were lost as residents tried to rescue animals from the areas that still had grazing land. The exceptionally high tide had breached the newly constructed embankments by 2 feet, a considerable amount of water, which covered the land from the docks to Cardiff Road.

# The Newport Transporter Bridge

There is a common denominator between Bow Bells and the transporter bridge. They say to be born within the sound of Bow Bells would identify as a Cockney. The Newport Transporter Bridge also identifies with a unique breed of people, the Newportonians. It has become a most eminent symbol of the city.

An unusual view of the gondola in this 1970 shot from the west bank.

The transporter bridge towers above a riot of terraced streets, signs and street furniture. Always in view, the bridge is a reassuring presence on the banks of the Usk.

For those like myself who were born in Pillgwenlly, the bridge was a part of our daily lives. The clanking and the steel-upon-steel soundtrack provided a backdrop to our lives. Even when not in immediate view, it could still be heard. The rhythmic motion as the trolley was dragged along the track could be likened to the trains that wound their way through the terraced housing.

The bridge was our playground. To the children of Pillgwenlly, this was our field of waving corn. Thick, unctuous mud formed by rising silt erupting from the seabed by the fastest of tides provided many an opportunity for play. Mud slides through broken glass and debris were the norm, as was the big swim, which involved hanging off the bottom of the bridge and dropping into the middle of the river for the swim back to the bank.

So, what is a transporter bridge? The bridge, or the Tranny as it is affectionately known, is a tower of steel and iron holding aloft a length of trackway, under which is suspended a car or gondolier. Described as an aerial carriageway, it has become iconic. It is a haven; a safe house of memory and experience for those who have experienced the pleasure of its presence.

Newport, Warrington and Middlesbrough each play host to a transporter bridge, as does Bilbao and Rochefort. There are just a few working bridges throughout the world, and elsewhere a number are in disrepair or have been demolished. In the UK, only Newport and Middlesbrough have working bridges.

A rare example of a transporter bridge originally designed for rail traffic still stands at Warrington in Cheshire. The bridge, which is now non-operational, has a strong 'Friends of Warrington Transporter Bridge' following working in its support. At the time of writing it is hoped that between the Friends and the local authorities, the bridge might one day be preserved, hopefully in a fully working state.

To the traveller, the very sight of these massive structures drew sharp intakes of breath, not to mention an attack of the vapours. A report shortly after the opening cited the reaction of those using the town's new electric trams. Circumnavigating Stow Hill at an astonishing 10 mph, passengers coming into first site of the gigantean transporter bridge would 'sink back in exhaustion' – obviously stunned witless by its grandeur ... or perhaps they had just been asked for their tram fare.

A low-level view of the gondola as it approaches Pillgwenlly.

The bridge is an experience of another age. The cage-like fence on the gondola and the iron-slatted seats create a sense of theatre. Is it a bridge, a ship, a fairground ride? Although not completed until the latter years of Victoria's reign, it has all the trappings of Victorian engineering at its best. Iron and steel, much of which would have been forged by hand, adorns every inch of the structure. As a Newportonian, I can happily say that, to me, it is Newport's Orient Express. It is a representation of our city that, both in the physical and psychological sense, stands above all else.

Mostly born in the shadow of the bridge, and seen standing in the shadows of the past in this 1974 picture, the residents of Wingate and Wolseley Street stand among the rubble as the mass redevelopment of their area, like the river, slowly surrounds them.

Middlesbrough Transporter Bridge, with its attendant mishmash of industries lining the quayside.

Runcorn's bridges come in pairs – two beautiful examples of industrial architecture. The transporter bridge is to the fore, and at the rear is the rail bridge.

Warrington Transporter Bridge was originally designed for carrying rail traffic linked with the petro-chemical industry.

The bridge at Marseille resembles the Newport bridge, apart from the hump in the main span. At the time of writing, I am unsure as to its working status.

An early engraving of the view over Newport before the construction of the bridge.

*Left*: When extreme weather closed the bridge and the trams ceased running, workers were faced with a 5-mile walk, often in blizzard conditions.

*Below*: The bridge, just visible before being engulfed in snow in 2009.

The bridge was a stalwart servant to the community. Only on rare occasions did it stop running, and it was usually the weather that was responsible. It was built primarily to connect the east and west banks at Pillgwenlly, providing connections to the steel plant of John Lysaght and the growing number of other industries in that area of the town.


## The Beginnings

It was reported in the *South Wales Daily News* on 11 October 1899 that parliamentary permission was to be sought for the construction of an overhead ferry, a provision for electricity for the tramway system and for the purchase of land and the building of a lunatic asylum, the latter at a cost of £80,000.

The need for an extra crossing of the Usk was dire. Whole new industries demanded workers and Pillgwenlly had the growing population to meet their demands. The river was a highway; tall ships still graced the banks and in later years massive liners and warships traversed the river en route to the numerous wharves and shipbreakers. Thus, the bridge must be tall enough to accommodate the ships that would pass beneath its main span.

Parliamentary consent was given in 1900 and work commenced in 1902. Having been under discussion since 1855, after forty years it had at last came to fruition. Much walking had been done in the meantime!


## The Ferryboat Disaster

Before the bridge there was a ferryboat. The Union Dock Company, on the opposite bank, employed over 100 men and the ferry company, comprising two boats, began to operate in 1986. Henry Dunn and Charlie Fowler were the boatmen, and would carry passengers to the boatyard for a sum of 1s per week – the equivalent of 5p today. This was not a popular move according to some who refused to pay, and when the money was taken from their wage packet, this caused further unrest. Eventually it was agreed that the trip would be funded by the firm.

The River Usk can be an unforgiving animal. The speed of its tide, and the mass of water at the point where it is near to the sea is often scary. When empty it resembles a huge basin – wide and gaping, with banks of oozing mud and silt. Those daring to voyage from its banks run a precarious route over wooden staging, which is both slippery and dangerous.

On the cold and foggy night of 18 January 1897, on a fast-incoming tide, the ferryboat left the dock on the east bank. Aboard were fifteen or more men. It had barely travelled 40 yards when an approaching tug, said to be travelling at an immense speed along the watery highway, created a wash that engulfed the boat and its passengers. The cries of the boatman to keep calm and remain still went unheeded; panic reigned and the boat was engulfed by the freezing water. The death and carnage that resulted would have far-reaching effects.

Prior to the planned bridge, the only means of crossing the Usk was via a ferryboat.

A surreal mudscape of deep peaks and troughs, enough to bury a small craft – or worse, a person. The boatmen on the Usk take this most difficult of terrain in their stride – or should it be wake?

Taken on 18 January 2018, we see similar conditions to the day of the great ferry disaster.

The direct result of a winter storm. Staging is sent into a concertina-shaped tangle by spring tides and storm-force winds.

*Left*: Worries were expressed at the planning stage over the jetties adjacent to the bridge. This resulted in the bridge being increased in width to avoid any infringment.

*Below*: On a cold January day, passengers well wrapped against the freezing fog alight on the Pillgwenlly side.

Swinging at anchor?
Three incredible views
of the SS *Conway*,
which is seen acting in
a very confused manner,
highlighting the thought
pattern on the infringment
of the adjacent warves.

*Left*: Slowly, the giant framework rises from the ground, resting on concrete anchorages each weighing 2,000 tons. This view is taken from Brunel Street.

*Below*: The designer and joint engineer was French engineer Ferdinand Arnodin. The construction was by Alfred Thorne of Westminster. It was opened in June 1906 by the Honourable Viscount Tredegar. The bridge has been witness to many historical events; here, one of the last sailing ships on the river, the *Edna Hoytt*, is heading for breaking up at Cashmore's.

## Facts, Ony Facts!

Had the studious Mr Gradgrind stepped out of the pages of Charles Dickens's *Hard Times*, he would have loved the transporter bridge, for was it not he who demanded 'Facts, only facts!'? The bridge is laden with facts.

For £90,000, one got a finished bridge. It has a travelling frame of 104 feet and has sixty wheels. The platform is 33 feet in length and 40 feet wide. The span is 645 feet and the clear headway from the underside of the span from high water is 177 feet. The height of the four towers is 242 feet and the anchorage weighs in an incredible 2,000 tons. When it comes to a daub of paint, one would need enough to cover an area of 44,000 square feet. It was decided that a charge would be made to cross, which was ½d.

Of course, in these scary days of global warming and rising tide levels, the working parameters could be severely challenged. Saying that, it is unlikely that we will see many more tall ships pass under this magnificent structure.

The Right Honourable Godfrey Charles Viscount Tredegar opened the bridge in 1906. A guard of honour comprising local volunteers lined the pavements, while hoots and whistles sounded to mark the achievement and what was to become a milestone in Newport's industrial heritage.

Shortly after opening there was controversy surrounding the charge levied by Newport Corporation. In April 1907 the *South Wales Daily News* reported that John Lysaght, who were strongly linked with the need for a bridge, were claiming £7,500 for

A very old and faded image of workmen posing on the top of the main span. I wonder how many were still in evidence after the photographer had uttered the immortal words, 'Back a little, please.'

WILLS'S CIGARETTES.

TRANSPORTER BRIDGE.

Wills's Cigarettes, whose cards provided us with colourful and collectable evidence of current events. Issued shortly after the opening of the bridge, the artwork strongly suggests that this is in fact the Newport Transporter Bridge.

crossing fees, which they ascertained were in breach of an agreement they made with Newport Corporation back in 1895. They claimed they were promised a free bridge. A settlement was later made out of court.

When opened, it was noticeable that the gates were missing from the gondola, only a chain protected travellers from the drop. I wonder when it was decided to offer this necessary security measure – probably when the Rolls-Royces began to appear in the mud.

The bridge has been a magnet for those seeking unusual publicity, including rock bands, actors, charitable groups fundraising by abseiling from the upper girders to name just a few. One of the more interesting groups who chose to be pictured in front of the monument was a transport touring group from the West of England. They and their vintage Royal Blue omnibus were enjoying their annual tour and couldn't resist a photo stop, with the bridge as their background.

The maintenance costs of keeping a 100-year-old transporter bridge working can be a drain on any local authority. As the first signs of long-term wear and tear were becoming known in the 1960s, there were serious doubts as to the future of the structure. An American businessman approached the town council with a view to purchasing the bridge and rebuilding it over the Grand Canyon. The resultant groundswell of local feeling was predictably negative.

Being on the bridge when things went wrong was not a pleasant experience. As children we constantly asked the question, 'Will it float when the cables snap and the whole thing drops into the river?' Will it float – I do believe they asked the same question of the *Titanic*. Yes, of course it will, we told ourselves as it lurched and groaned from bank to bank, often just a few feet above the highest water levels. On one occasion in the early 1980s, when taking a shortcut during the daily school run, the bridge

A tantalising glimpse of the past: sail and steam at Newport.

Mostly sails in view when this was taken, just after the 1906 opening.

Those brave enough to ascend to the top are afforded generous views of the Alexandra Dock and the Bristol Channel.

Ghosts of the past rise from the mud. Here, we see the Tredegar Dry Dock, the Uskside Iron Foundry and the plethora of terraced homes that housed the workforce that breathed life into Newport's earliest industries.

A tour in a Royal Blue coach – what could be better?

Rust and corrosion at the very top of the structure.

'Will it float when the cables snap and the whole thing drops into the river?'

The bridge today. Prior to the refurbishment of the 1990s, the bridge was a noisy entity that could be heard throughout Pilgwenlly.

shuddered and ground to a halt midstream, leaving us swinging precariously above the river. We were told that the carriage, high above us, had been derailed, and we sat for over an hour while workmen with sledgehammers drove it back onto its rails.

In the late 1980s a major refurbishment was commissioned; the bridge had been designated an item of special scientific and historic interest and a date was set to start the refurbishment. This was the year 1992 and the official reopening of the bridge was planned for 1995. Money from CADW, the EC, Gwent County Council and the Welsh Office allowed the work to commence. It would be a long and costly process.

At the outset of the work, I undertook to take progress pictures of the mass of scaffolding that was soon to cover the structure. After just a few steps to the upper levels, I was prevented from going any further. The reason quoted to me was that the steelwork was paper-thin in places, and it was far too dangerous to proceed. Only a small number of key personnel were allowed to make the hazardous journey at that time.

The sheer elegance of the gondola is often lost on those who see the bridge on a daily basis. The whole roadbed, if placed on water, would not look unlike a chain ferry, the likes of which are found on the River Dart or the Tamar.

When Arnodin built the bridge, the styles of the structure and gondola would have been commonplace, especially in Britain. I am quite sure that the elegant industrial architecture of the much lamented Isambard Kingdom Brunel might have been an influential factor to many of the world's greatest engineers.

Rust and corrosion was the make-up worn by this grand old lady in 1992. The steelwork was as thin as paper in places.

Flaking paint and rusting metal attack the
thousands of rivets in this top girder.

When this image was taken in 1974, the
bridge was as most of us remembered
it – a spindly, rusting old friend with more
than a touch of mechanical arthritis.

*Right*: Taken from the east bank, on which John Lysaught's was situated, the sign warns of submerged gas pipes. 'Do not anchor between the signs!' it proclaims. Who would want to anchor in the path of a moving transporter bridge?

*Below*: Scaffolding poles and planking litter the roadway. The gondola hangs in a forlorn and tired state. The workmen are no longer passengers but are in residence as the mammoth task of refurbishment gets underway.

While the gondola could be confused as a ferryboat, the control tower could be seen as a railway signal box. Add a few extra sections and I see Clapham Junction, with the over-track signal box that straddled the mass of railway lines.

The bridge as it was in 2015, bathed in sunshine and with paintwork seemingly intact. It was common for the kids to hang on to the framework below the platform and drop into the deep waters of the Usk, before swimming back to the bank. This was an incredible act of strength but also stupidity, as the tide in the river could be lethal.

Now covered in scaffolding, the refurbishment could begin in earnest.

Lighting in the 1990s created a ghostly vision of the steelwork.

The bridge has been illuminated on a number of occasion, not always with success, as the bulbs had been stolen and the cost of running the lights has come into question.

After many years the work was completed and the bridge was reopened on 15 December 1995 by Claire Short MP. It was a cold, dark winter night, with patches of fine, stinging rain. The celebrations were hardly on par with the great official opening of 1906. Much political rhetoric was in the air, and I felt great disappointment that such a happy occasion was, in my opinion, marred by such talk.

There appears to have been a constant dialogue in process since the 1960s relating to the costs of repairing the bridge and whether it would be better to demolish or sell it. Happily, events have worked in the favour of the bridge and it has now become an iconic artefact depicting Newport and its heritage. It is supported by an active 'Friends of' group and whatever happens it will always have the love and respect of the Newport community.

# The Lost Industries on the Banks of the Usk

It is said that where there is muck, there is brass. It can equally be stated that where there is water, there will be a dock. The oldest structure on the banks of the Usk will be the castle. Robert, Earl of Gloucester, lived there in 1147, but it is believed that a simple wooden structure existed prior to that. Castles are not built overnight.

Clearly it was the first major point of trade, as the humdrum of medieval life would have been focused on the castle and whoever was in residence at that point in history. The river, which would not have been as polluted as there was no industry, would no doubt have been fished as a food source and for trade. It was also a crossing point, initially by ford and then a bridge built by the Normans. The principle trading port on the river was then Caerleon. Wool from Llantarnam was in great demand and ships carrying other goods, such as iron, regularly sailed across to Bristol and North Somerset.

The watergate of Newport Castle, a secure stronghold for incomings via the river. The castle also had a moat, which was 24 feet wide and 12 feet deep. Behind the watergate there was a dock of sorts, where visiting craft discharged their cargo.

The components of a thriving community. The corner shop, the local pub and behind is the spire of the Catholic Church. Out of view and behind the houses was the huge Uskside engineering works. And, of course, the river.

A firm favourite is the West of England pub, pictured literally in the shadows of the transporter bridge. Being at the entrance to the docks and the bridge, this fine pub was at one time one of the busiest in town.

While looking at the lost industries on the river, we must consider venues such as the pubs and corner shop, for without the communities and the employment that the river gave, they would not exist. It is sad to say that at the time of writing there are no longer corner or front-room shops, while the dockland pub is all but finished.

## Mordey, Carney & Co.

The dry docks of Mordey, Carney & Co., who were one of the larger shipbuilders on the river, opened in 1890. Between the transporter bridge and the town bridge, there were nearly forty wharves. Shipbuilding and repair was prolific, and in 1835 there were no less than seven vessels on the stocks in Newport, but it was the discovery of the Newport Ship that showed us Newport's real shipbuilding gem.

## Atlantic Shipbuilding

Newport's shipbuilding enterprises were mostly small and river-based. Founded in 1953 by the Bailey family, a new company, Atlantic Shipbuilding, was founded and employed

Dry docks on the river opposite Dock Street station (seen to the left).

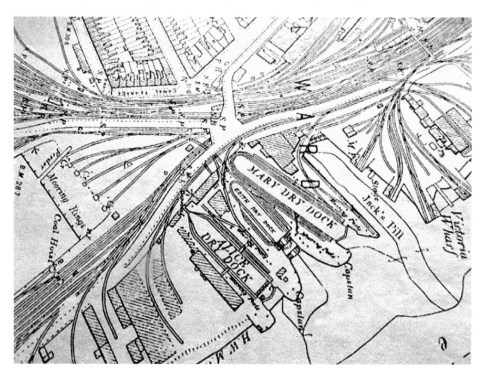

The Alice, Mary and Edith graving docks.

The *Oceana* in the Mordey, Carney & Co. shipyard (close to Jack's Pill).

The same scene today can only be described as incredibly drab, with architecture that would not look out of place in any Russian post-war city; little boxes, little windows. Populating the riverbank has certainly improved the outlook, but does it look like something very exciting is going on?

The *Matanzus* undergoing sea trials in the Bristol Channel.

Often, vessels were built in pairs from fabricated sections – man-sized Meccano!

The *Pina Del Rio* being fitted out in the Alexandra Dock.

The two ships are towed by tug into the Alexandra Dock for fitting out.

Not the best composed image in the world, but it clearly shows the location and the Newport Power Station at the mouth of the river.

over 250 personnel. Situated on the Alexandra Dock with a lock opening near the mouth of the Usk, much larger ships were able to be built, launched and then brought into the dock for fitting out. The company subsequently received commissions for three vessels to be used on the Great Lakes by a Canadian trading company, with trawlers for British and Ghanaian companies following soon after. In the 1960s the firm ran into difficulties, being restructured and renamed the Newport Shipbuilding Company. It ceased trading in 1966.

## P&A Campbell

Passenger ships have made a brief appearance once more at Newport, but passenger traffic is not a new concept. P&A Campbell have been gracing the river for over 100 years with their paddleboats and pleasure steamers. Originally from Scotland, they were later based in Bristol, where they became the principle operators of paddle steamers in the Bristol Channel.

The Bristol Packet that sailed from her wharf adjacent to the town bridge was a commercial fare-paying service. She called at Pillgwenlly en route to the West Country, with the return fare being a shilling. Early maps show that her dropping-off point was Campbell's pier, which was close to the entrance to the Old Dock.

Sailing on the *Waverley*, one of the oldest paddle steamers afloat.

The *Balmoral*, a regular visitor to the Usk and Newport. The P&O Campbell boats once sailed from the centre of town, but the lack of landing facilities have seen them move further down the river, to the dock. Part of the charm of a trip to Steep or Flat Holme was the river journey – it made us feel quite posh!

Here, the *Albion* passes what is probably Canal Parade. St Woolos Cathedral is seen in the background.

Taken in the 1800s near the grid iron and the pontoon. To the left is the premises of the Water Company.

Adjacent to the Town Bridge was the departure point for the Bristol Packet.

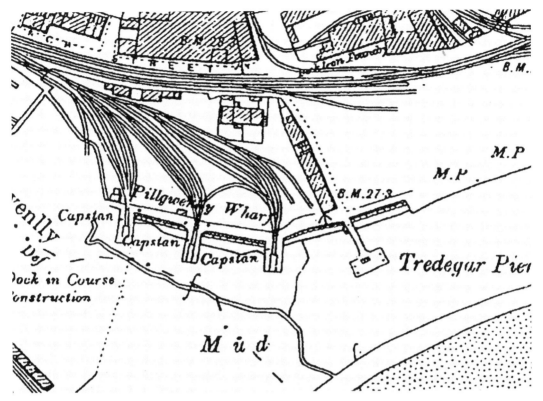

The Tredegar Pier, just on the town side of the Town Dock, leading on to Church Street. The map shows the site of the Tredegar Dry Dock, which at this point is under construction.

Taken from the *Johns' Directory* of 1882, this is an advertisement for the Steam Packet Co.

A late Victorian postcard describes this as the Newport Pier. The description given in Campbell's guide suggests that this is in fact the passenger pier in Pillgwenlly and the craft might well be the Bristol Packet, as seen advertised on page 58.

The Ship and Pilot. This could have been the first port of call for passengers alighting at the Tredegar/Campbell pier.

A childhood joy was to see the ships in the Tredegar Dry Dock, angled in such a way that it gave the impression that the ship was actually about to meet the No. 9 bus in Commercial Road.

The 1907 P&A Campbell guide describes a sea journey from Newport to Minehead: 'The River Usk looks well this morning … On the way down we call at Tredegar Pier, built for the convenience of the lower portion of the town by P&A Campbell, to take on extra passengers.'

## On the East Bank

The greater part of Newport's riverside industries were on the Pillgwenlly side, which was probably due to the canal and the railway link. There were, however, some notable dock facilities on the opposite bank. The Union Dock Company, largely featured in the ferryboat disaster, became known as the Severn Dry Docks (1905) and in 1916 was listed as the Channel Dry Docks. This has seen numerous occupiers and is currently used for the shipment of scrap metals. It might be remembered as the Bell Ferry Terminal from the 1970s.

The Eastern Dry Dock in the early 1980s.

Over thirty years later, the only difference is the lack of a dock crane on the south lock of the Alexandra Dock.

## The Foundries and the Great Works

## John Lysaght Ltd

The gatehouse.

The largest of all the industries on the Usk was the steel plant belonging to John Lysaght. John Lysaght Iron & Steel was founded in Bristol in 1857, but developed works in Newport, Wolverhampton and Scunthorpe. In 1920 the company was acquired by Guest, Keen & Nettlefolds, which is still one of the biggest British steel companies. The works as it was closed in recent years, and a steadily growing housing estate now occupies much of the riverbank.

In the 1980s, Lysaght's landing stage was still very active. Behind is the much-loved Lysaght Institute.

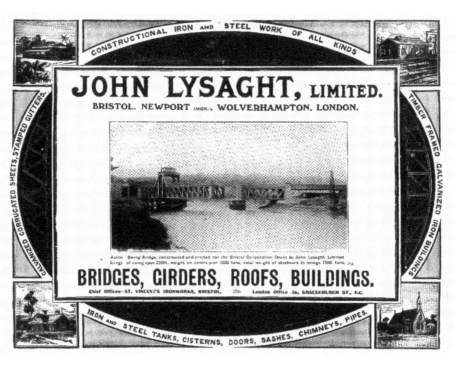

An advertisement for John Lysaght, based in Newport, Bristol, Wolverhampton and London.

## Braithwaites

Located next to the transporter bridge, Braithwaites are a Newport company with a truly international reputation. Most of us will have come across the work of this company and probably never realised it. The tell-tale design of their water tanks can still be seen in all parts of the country. However, heavy engineering and steelworks were their main point of business, and much of their work can still be seen in what remains of Newport's industrial domain.

A rarely seen view of the first Newport Power Station on the banks of the Usk. It also shows Holy Cross RC School on the Pill side of the river. The steelworks were constructed by Braithwaite.

As seen from the west bank, Newport Corporation omnibuses are parked to the left of the structure.

The omnibus garage on Corporation Road, using steel roof supports by Braithwaite and the station canopies of Newport High Street. Note the fleet of single-deck buses. (Thanks to Andrew Hoppe of Braithwaite.)

## C. H. Bailey Tyne, Engine Works

C. H. Bailey is a name synonymous to South Wales and to this day their head office is still in Newport. They were founded in 1888 and specialised in dry docks, ship repairing, and heavy engineering. The Tyne Engine Works was in Mill Parade, close to the Alexandra Dock and transporter bridge.

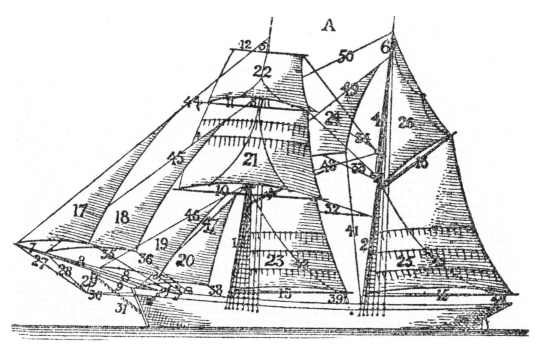

The extent of this company's comprehensive range of services is demonstrated in the C. H. Bailey *Book of Useful Information*. This tiny, green, hard-backed booklet of over 300 pages is indeed a bible, for it details virtually every core component of a steam ship, sailing ship, windlass, valves, packing, steam chest and even railway lines for every company in Britain. It is a tribute to those who started the company, and their knowledge of engineering in that period is indeed enviable.

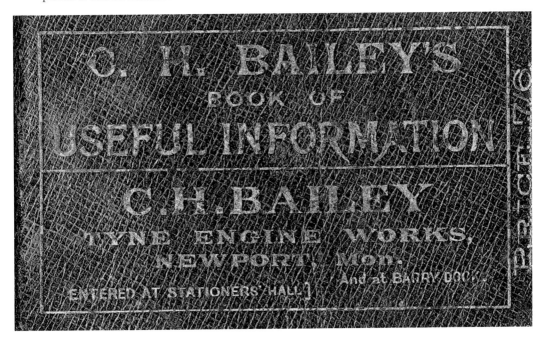

The building has had a number of uses since the Tyne Works closed, but the classic image of the works, when it was a young lad's dream to hitch a ride on the side of the engine, is timeless.

## Uskside Iron Foundry and Engineering

In its later years the company became NEWELCO. Sadly it is now closed, like so much of Britain's engineering works. Here it is shown in happier times, with much happening on the shop floor. Today the site is used for storage units.

Founded in 1827 by William Evans as a blacksmiths, the Uskside Iron Foundry & Engineering has remained on the same site, by the side of the Usk. It originally made anchors and chains, but over time moved into heavy engineering. Around 1852 it became an ironworks and was purchased by one John Evans. Evans eventually moved to Russia with several Welsh steel and ironworkers and founded a highly successful steelworks, which eventually led to the town being named after him. In the late 1800s, when the company needed to expand, they purchased half a street (Speedwell Street) from Newport Borough Council. The building remained intact until recently.

You can feel the heat and smell the oil in this slightly older image.

## Black Clawson

The Black Clawson wharf as it is today.

Two images at the same location, one showing happier times, and the other sad and forlorn with derelict buildings. New houses now stand in its place. Albeit no longer on the banks of the Usk, the successful company lives on!

Black Clawson produced machinery used in the paper and card industry. It had its own river wharf and was near to the Old Town Dock. It had a very good social club, which for many years was run by a popular local family, the Seftons. The company originated in the USA and came to Newport in 1948. It was not the oldest company on the Usk, but it played its part in the lives of those who worked and lived nearby. This is an aerial view of the site, which also shows the site of the Old Town Dock (the large green area) and what was known as Spittle's Point, named as such because of Spittle's Foundry.

## John Cashmore, Shipbreakers

The Cashmore yard was a living history lesson. Unlike the nearby Dai Woodham's of Barry, whose speciality was railway stock, the sheer variety found at Cashmore's was immense, comprising ocean liners, warships, submarines and railway stock from all ages. A Staffordshire company founded in 1872, it had its main office in Tipton. Shipbreaking ceased in October 1976, and the last vessels to be seen were submarines. Additionally, many hundreds of steam locomotives met their end in Cashmore's yard. The site has now completely vanished and is occupied by new houses.

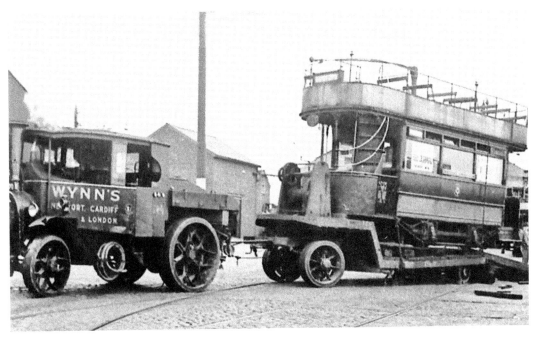

Here, a Wynn's solid-tyre low-loader delivers an old Newport Tram to Cashmore's for scrapping. In those halcyon days, Newport firms used Newport firms. It was a network of support and co-operation.

No sentiment shown as man's most faithful servant, the steam locomotive, is lined up for the cutting torch.

It was not all work in the 1950s as Cashmore's staff are photographed at Newport station. The poster in the background advertises camping coaches, a unique form of seaside holiday from another generation.

Another vessel heading to the Newport graveyard. I feel a Doric moment coming on!

THIS **LINER** WILL BE

# OPEN FOR PUBLIC INSPECTION

FROM

## FRIDAY 15th TO SATURDAY 23rd NOVEMBER, 1935,

On behalf of the

# ROYAL GWENT HOSPITAL
# SPECIAL APPEAL FUND.

FIRST AUCTION SALE OF FURNISHINGS will take place on
NOVEMBER 26th, 27th, 28th, 29th, 1935.

# JOHN CASHMORE Ltd., Shipbreakers, NEWPORT, Mon.

When the liners came in, the furnishings were sold to the public, but scenes that could have come straight from the pages of *Whisky Galore* were commonplace, as doors and wardroom tables appeared in the darkened streets of Pillgwenlly.

Cashmore's yard at Newport, as well as the coal distribution yard. This was also the site of the original Dock Street railway station.

## James Mahoney, Rope, Oakum, Canvas, Iron and Metal Merchants

James Mahoney & Co. Ltd.

Tom White.
I interviewed Tom some years ago. He was a softly spoken man of great experience and knowledge, who gave me the history of the company and its activity. He spoke of salvaged hemp ropes, which were dried and then sold to the Americans, who turned them into quality brown paper. 'Money for old rope', he laughed.

Mahoney's yard was accessed via Portland Street, but had a variety of storage facilities in the area, including at the Old Town Dock. Pictured here in 1907 is HMS *Montague*, which had run aground off Lundy in the Bristol Channel. Unable to re-float her, she was part purchased by Mahoney's and was broken up on-site. Much of her scrap ended up in their yard in Newport.

## Boats, Trains and Automobiles: The Continuing Story of Scrap

The ritualistic dance of the dead Volkswagen, void of all useful bits and waiting patiently for the torch.

The 1970s was probably the last decade of the old river. Sad, tired wharves, a number of old lifeboats sit next to the distant staging, probably once used to collect river coal, while fading into the fog in accord with the diminishing scene, a small coaster unloads coal onto one of the remaining timber wharves. However, one man's junk is another man's treasure, and the scrapping and salvage of cars and vans was a feature until the end. It was not always attractive, but that is the way it was; a part of everyday life.

## Old King Coal

Gwent Coal Distribution and Lower Dock Street.

Industry was all about coal; it powered the railways, the factories, the ships and the foundries. It sustained us, and communities made their living from coal.

The Gwent Coal Distribution depot at Dock Street had its own small diesel locomotive for moving loaded coal hoppers.

The coal arrived from all directions. Here, a coal train from the Western Valleys passes Whitehead Steelworks en route to the docks.

A very old image of a riverbank coal yard, with handcarts, hats and coal.

Coal trimmers pose for the camera. The poor little lad on the end! The shovel is bigger than he was at that time.

## MACHEN WHARF,
### or 39 Mill Parade,
#### NEWPORT,
190

Mr.

DEAR SIR,

We beg to call your attention to the following Price List for House Coals.

You will find **the prices compare favourably with any that can be offered elsewhere.** We assure you **the quality is equally favourable.**

We should be glad to give special quotations for large quantities

We can deliver the Coal in bags if required.

We remain,

Yours faithfully,

# James Parry & Sons.

A notice from James Parry of Machen Warf: favourable prices for house coal – what else would one expect?

## The Maltings

Newport had many breweries, a large percentage of which were in the docklands. Here we see the Maltings, which had ultra-low ceilings in the drying rooms for the hops. It stood on the lower end of the Old Town Dock and was destined for a refurbishment and a new lease of life as a modern development, but sadly it caught fire and was severely damaged.

## The Tredegar Dry Dock

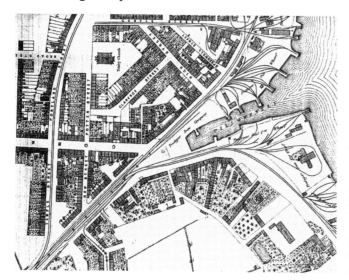

The Tredegar Dry Dock was opened in 1902. It was built on the Pill, from which Pillgwenlly took it name. Here we see the original village of Pillgwenlly, a small group of cottages on the marshes. Newport was as far away as the moon.

## The Foundries

By the early 1900s Newport had a dozen or more iron or brass foundries of varying sizes. Even today many items of street furniture can be seen carrying the maker's name. Pictured here in Church Street is the remains of the brass foundry, parts of which are still used today as a community facility.

## The Baltic Oil Company

There are many Baltic wharves throughout the country and I can only assume that as they are all dock- and shipping-related, they were used as a point of trade with the Baltic regions. The Baltic Oil Company has been on the Old Dock almost since it was built and must be the only original building of its age still in use in the city. This building has much going for it, with drystone walls, brick arches, iron bars and the vintage railway oil tanks that stand as, I assume, extra storage still in existence.

The date over the main entrance says '1844', which if true means that it will definitely fit into the 'long white beard' category.

Built in the year that the YMCA was founded and Charles Goodyear patented the vulcanising of rubber, the Baltic Oil Company is still purveying oil products to this day.

Dry-stone walling and railway heritage are abound in these two images. Here, ex-GW six-wheeled oil tanks have spent their retirement years at the Baltic, being used as storage. One could easily still be in the nineteenth century.

After many years of various usage, this aged gem is offering up her secrets. Under the words 'Henry Morris', a new clue as to its identity has appeared.

## The Fishermen

It is difficult to calculate how many years there has been a fishing industry in Newport, but it is fair to say that as long as there has been salmon, cod and flatfish, there have been fisherman. Today, with licenses all but non-existent, it has become a part of history.

The Sully family, drying their fishing nets.

In 2003 a calendar was produced in celebration of salmon fishing when the licence to fish was brought into question.

## The Town Reach

The Town Reach is the area between George Street Bridge, built in 1963, and Newport Bridge, which stands next to the castle. Located here were many industries, including Ansell's breweries, the flour mills and the Sessions sand wharves, to name just three. The last to trade were Sessions, who used small boats to unload sand that had been dredged from the river into the wharf in readiness for use in the construction industry.

The final chapter of commercial life as it was on the Usk came when Lysaght's, Black Clawson and the remaining coal wharf became inactive. The Old Dock is flanked by new roads, housing a car dealer and a gastro pub, and the maltings stand as a burnt-out shell. There are still traders on the riverbanks, but few share the knowledge that their forefathers were pioneers in the great industrial theatre of dreams that became the city of Newport as it stands today.

The George Street Bridge, a great viewpoint from which to gaze upon nothing. To its right is the warehouse of Thomas Ward of Sheffield.

Cranes line the banks, Ansell's and Sessions sand are prominent, and small coastal craft wait to be offloaded. In the distance is, as usual, the transporter bridge.

The sand hopper at Sessions is now empty and the riverbanks are being stripped of their history in favour of inglorious plastic bingo halls and characterless pods in which humanity is expected, for some strange reason, to be happy.

# The End of an Era

Hard to believe that those travelling on these rusting tracks could have once been heading for the North of England. Dock Street station, the Octopus Bridge and Cashmore's would have all been part of the greater plan, as was the Old Town Dock, all of which was accessed at this point, in Lower Dock Street.

The final chapter of commercial life as it was on the Usk came when Lysaght's, Black Clawson and the remaining coal wharf became inactive. The old dock is flanked by new roads, housing a car dealer and a gastro pub. The Maltings stand as a burnt-out shell. There are still traders on the riverbanks, but few still share the knowledge that their forefathers were pioneers in the great industrial theatre of dreams which became the city of Newport as it stands today.

Two of the last commercial visitors to the river. Lysaght's Wharf is in the background, as are the blast furnaces of the Llanwern Steelworks, which has now in part been decommissioned.

The sun has set on the riverbank industries, and the terraced streets and corner shops that were synonymous with the city have become but names in the history book. Perhaps in another time someone will write about life on the banks of the Usk in the twenty-first century, but I doubt if they will have much to say.

# Acknowledgements

While compiling this book, it has become acutely aware to me that there is much more to the bridge than iron and steel. There is an underlying sense of community and ownership, which has identified the bridge as Newport's own.

Since the days of the Pill Heritage Centre, I have been moved by the amount of information and images that are still offered in support of my efforts here in Pillgwenlly, for which I thank you. I have taken every effort to ascertain copyright and permissions for images used in this publication. I would like to offer my special thanks to the following:

Duncan Brown, Councillor Charles Ferris, the late Cliff Knight, the late Terry Underwood, Doug Parker, Jim O'Neill, Andrew Hoppe of Braithwaites, Don Carter of the Gwent Family History Society, and Ron Inglis (formerly of Newport Museum Services).

My thanks also to the following organisations and sources: Black Clawson, Jan Preece Heritage Collection & Picture Library, Newport City Council, Newport Museum Services, Friends of Warrington Transporter Bridge, Uskside Engineering Company, the British Newspaper Archive, the *Cardiff and South Wales Weekly News*, the *South Wales Argus*, the *South Wales Daily News*, the *Monmouthshire Merlin*, the *Monmouthshire Beacon*, Mercantile Marine, Historic Newport (Matthews), Local Government in Newport (Warner) and *Johns' Directory* (1884).